GITA

Gandhi's Letters on the *Bhagavad Gita*

Mohandas K. Gandhi

BANDANNA BOOKS   1989   SANTA BARBARA

Reprinted by permission of Navajivan Trust, Ahmedabad-380 014 (India). For information contact Bandanna Books, 319-B Anacapa Street, Santa Barbara, CA 93101.

HUMANIST CLASSICS FROM BANDANNA BOOKS

Walt Whitman, Original 1855 Edition of *Leaves of Grass*, with the 1855 Preface. Reset from Whitman's original text. Modernized by A.S. Ash. ISBN 0-942208-08-0 $8.00

John Milton, *Areopagitica, Freedom of the Press*. A classic in the history of censorship. ISBN 0-942208-04-8 $5.00

Sappho, the Poems, revised edition, translated and with an introduction by Sasha Newborn. ISBN 0-942208-11-0 $5.00

Apology of Socrates, with Crito, Plato, in Benjamin Jowett's 1864 translation. The trial of Socrates. ISBN 0-942208-05-6 $5.00

Dante and His Circle, D.G. Rossetti's collection of love poetry by 14 poets of the early Renaissance, including Guido Cavalcanti, Boccaccio and Giotto. With Dante's *Vita Nuova*. Modernized, with introduction by A.S. Ash. ISBN 0-942208-09-9 $9.00

ALSO AVAILABLE

Steven Posusta's *Don't Panic: The Procrastinator's Guide to Writing an Effective Term Paper*. A college essential for writing. 64pp. ISBN 0-942208-42-0 $6.95

Charlotte Perkins Gilman, *Benigna Machiavelli*. Novel of adolescence by the author of "The Yellow Wallpaper." Introduction by Joan Blake. ISBN 0-942208-18-8 $10.00

Ghazals of Ghalib, tr. Sasha Newborn. Ironic verse of the Moghul poet. ISBN 0-942208-06-4 $7.00

The Little Gospel, Leo Tolstoy, with Tolstoy's anti-church introduction, tr. Sasha Newborn. ISBN 0-942208-02-1 $11.00

Surfing: A Royal Sport, Jack London. London discovered surfing in Hawaii in 1911. 20pp. ISBN 0-942208-12-9 $2.00

Italian for Opera Lovers, ed. Hassan W. Ebron. Terms and definitions, pronunciation guide. ISBN 0-942208-17-X $3.50

Second printing 1996
ISBN 0-942208-03-X   LC 86-64055

EDITOR'S INTRODUCTION

Gandhi's translation of the *Bhagavad Gita* into his native Gujarati had just been published in 1930. Then, while he was serving a two-year sentence in Yeravda Central Prison, he received a letter from a member of his own *ashram* (community) complaining that the new translation was very difficult to understand. Gandhi replied, and then expanded his commentary into a series of letters, one on each chapter. *Gandhi on the Gita: Gandhi's Letters on the Bhagavad Gita* allows a prolonged look at the mature ethical thinking of Mohandas K. Gandhi.

The *Bhagavad Gita* was written as a dialogue between the warrior Arjuna and his charioteer, the god Krishna, just as they have stationed themselves between two armies about to attack each other. Arjuna, with relatives on both sides, has moral doubts about taking part in the battle. Lord Krishna answers Arjuna's doubts one by one.

The humanist pronouns *hu, hus, hum,* familiar to readers of other titles in the Humanist Classics series, are not used in the text of this book, so that fidelity to prior editions, which are protected by existing copyright, may be maintained.

Sasha Newborn
Santa Barbara, 1989

TO THE READER

I would like to say to the diligent reader of my writings and to others who are interested in them that I am not at all concerned with appearing to be consistent. In my search after Truth I have discarded many ideas and learnt many new things. Old as I am in age, I have no feeling that I have ceased to grow inwardly or that my growth will stop at the dissolution of the flesh. What I am concerned with is my readiness to obey the call of Truth, my God, from moment to moment, and, therefore, when anybody finds any inconsistency between any two writings of mine, if he has still faith in my sanity, he would do well to choose the later of the two on the same subject.

M. K. Gandhi
Harijan, 29-4-'33

CHAPTER ONE

The *Gita* is a small portion of the *Mahabharata*. The latter is generally looked upon as a historical work. To us, however, the *Mahabharata* and the *Ramayana* are not historical works but are treatises on religion. Or, if we call them histories, they narrate the history of the human soul; they do not tell of what happened thousands of years ago, but depict what takes place in the heart of every human being today. Both the works describe the eternal war between the God and the demon in man—between Rama and Ravana. The *Gita* does this in the form of a dialogue between Arjuna and Krishna. The dialogue is narrated to the blind Shritarashtra by Sanjaya. Literally *Gita* means that which is sung. The adjective applies to the noun *Upanishad*, which is understood, and so the full meaning of the phrase is "the Upanishad which was sung." *Upanishad* means knowledge-teaching. The word *Gita*, therefore, means Shri Krishna's teaching to Arjuna. In reading the *Gita* we should feel that Shri Krishna—God—dwells in our hearts as the holy spirit within us, and that when, yearning for knowledge, like Arjuna, we take our spiritual difficulties to Him and seek His guidance, seek refuge in Him, He is ever ready to instruct us. We slumber, but the Lord within us is ever awake. He is only waiting for spiritual yearning to be awakened in us. We, however, do not know how to question Him, do not even feel the desire to do so. And so we read a work like the *Gita* every day and meditate over its teaching. By doing so, we wish to awaken spiritual yearning in us and learn what questions to put to the Lord. Whenever we are faced with spiritual difficulties, we turn to the *Gita* for their solution and obtain peace of mind through it. This is the spirit in which we should read the work. It is as it were our revered guru, our mother, and we should have faith that we shall be safe if we seek shelter in her lap. We can get all our spiritual difficulties solved through the *Gita*. Anyone who daily meditates over the teaching of the *Gita* in this manner will ever experience new joy in his study and find new meanings. There is no spiritual problem which the *Gita* cannot solve, though it may be that owing to our imperfect faith we do not know how to read and understand the work. We read the *Gita* as daily spiritual practice so that our faith may increase from day to day and we may become vigilant. I give here, for the guidance of the inmates of the Ashram, the meaning of the *Gita* which my daily meditation over its teaching has revealed or reveals to me.

When the Pandavas and the Kauravas gathered together on the battlefield of *Kurukshetra* (the field of Kuru) with their armies, Duryodhana, the king of the Kauravas, approached Drona (his teacher in the science of war) and named the leading warriors on either side. As a signal for the battle to begin, conchshell horns were sounded on both the sides and Shri Krishna, who was Arjuna's charioteer, drove his chariot into a place between the two armies. The scene which greeted Arjuna's eyes unnerved him, and he said to Shri Krishna, "How can I attack these in battle? I might fight readily enough if I had to fight with strangers, but these are my kinsmen. The Kauravas and the Pandavas are first cousins. We were brought up together. Drona is our teacher as well as the Kauravas'. Bhishma is a revered elder for both. How can I fight with him? It is true that the Kauravas are criminals and doers of evil deeds. They have wronged the Pandavas and deprived them of their lands. They have insulted Draupadi. But what shall I gain by killing them? They are fools indeed. But shall I also be equally foolish? I have some little knowledge. I can discriminate between right and wrong. I thus see that it is a sin to fight with relatives. Never mind if they have taken wrongful possession of the Pandavas' share in the kingdom. Never mind even if they kill us.

"But how dare we raise our hand against them? O Krishna, I will not fight with my kith and kin."

With these words, Arjuna sank down on the seat of the chariot, being overwhelmed with grief.

Here ends the first Chapter which is entitled "the sorrow of Arjuna." All of us should feel pain even as Arjuna did. No acquisition of knowledge is possible unless there is in us a sense of something lacking and a desire to know the truth. If a man is not curious even to know what is wrong and what is right, what is the use of religion for him? The battlefield of Kurukshetra only provides the occasion for the dialogue between Arjuna and Krishna. The real Kurukshetra is the human heart, which is also a *dharmakshetra* (the field of righteousness) if we look upon it as the abode of God and invite Him to take hold of it. Some battle or other is fought on this battlefield from day to day. Most of these battles arise from the distinction between "mine" and "thine," between kinsmen and strangers. Therefore, as we shall find later on, the Lord tells Arjuna that attraction (*raga*) and repulsion (*dvesha*) lie at the root of sin. When I look upon a person or thing as "mine," raga takes hold of my mind; and when I look upon him as a stranger, aversion or hatred enters the mind.

Therefore we must forget the distinction between "mine" and "thine." That is to say, we must give up our likes and dislikes. This is the teaching of the *Gita* and all other scriptures. To say this is one thing; to practice it is quite another. The *Gita* is there to teach us how to practice it. We will try to understand the method it recommends.

CHAPTER TWO

When Arjuna had picked himself up a little bit, the Lord rebuked him and said, "How is it that this delusion has come to you? It is unworthy of a warrior like you." But even then Arjuna stuck to his first position, refused to fight and said, "If in order to get it, I have to slay elders and other relations, I do not want not only a kingdom on this earth but even the delights of paradise. My mind gropes in darkness. I do not know where my duty lies. I put myself into your hands. Please guide me."

Finding that Arjuna was bewildered and aspired after knowledge, Krishna had pity on him and proceeded to explain things to him: "Your sorrow is for nothing, and you utter words about wisdom without understanding. You have evidently forgotten the distinction between the body and the embodied soul. The soul never dies; but the body passes through childhood, youth and age and perishes in the end. The body is born but the soul is birthless and unchanging. It ever was, is now and will be there for all time to come. For whom then do you grieve? Your grief arises from a delusion. You look upon these Kauravas as your own, but you are aware that their bodies will come to an end. And as for the souls which inhabit these bodies, no one can destroy them. The soul cannot be wounded by weapons, burned by fire, dried by the wind or drowned in water. Then again, consider this from the standpoint of your duty as a warrior with an army under his command. If you refuse to fight this righteous war, the consequences will be the very reverse of what you expect and you will become an object of ridicule. You have always enjoyed the reputation of being a brave man. But if now you withdraw from the battle, you will be supposed to have been driven from it by fear. If it were part of your duty to flee in the face of danger, disgrace would not matter, but if you retire from battle now, you will have failed to discharge your duty, and people will be justified in condemning your flight.

"Thus far, I have tried to reason out things, draw a distinction between the body and the soul and remind you of your duty as a warrior. But let me now explain *Karmayoga* (the method of action). A practitioner of Karmayoga never comes to harm. It has nothing to do with chopping logic. It is something to be translated into action and experience. An ounce of practice is more profitable than tons of argumentation. And this practice too must not be vitiated by speculation about its fruit. Literalists perform Vedic rites directed to the acquisition of material rewards. If one rite does not yield the expected fruit, they have recourse to another, and being disappointed once more, they take up a third. And thus they suffer from utter mental confusion. As a matter of fact, it is up to us to do our duty without wasting a single thought on the fruits of our action. To fight is the duty you have to discharge at present. Gain or loss, defeat or victory, is not in your power. Why should you carry the needless burden of thinking about them and be like the dog who walks under a cart and imagines that it is being drawn by himself and not by the bullocks? Defeat and victory, heat and cold, pleasure and pain come to a man in turn and he must put up with them. Without worrying about the fruit of action, a man must devote himself to the performance of his duty with an evenness of temper. This is yoga, or skill in action. The success of an act lies in performing it, and not in its result, whatever it is. Therefore be calm and do your duty clear of consequences."

On hearing all this Arjuna said, "The course of conduct you have mapped for me seems to be beyond my capacity. Not to worry about defeat or victory, not to waste a thought on the result—how can one attain such an evenness of temper and steadfastness in spirit? How does a man with such attainments behave, and how are we to recognize him?"

The Lord replied, "O king, one who renounces all the cravings which torment the heart and derives his contentment from within himself is said to be a *sthitaprajna* or *samadhistha* (one stable in spirit). He is unruffled in adversity, and he does not hanker after happiness. Pleasure and pain are felt through the five senses. Therefore this wise man draws his senses away from sense objects even as a tortoise draws in his limbs. The tortoise withdraws into his shell when he apprehends danger. But in the case of human beings sense objects are ready to attack the senses at all times; therefore their sense must always be drawn in, and they should be ever ready to fight against sense objects. This is the real battle. Some people resort to self-mortification and fasting as weapons of defense against sense objects. These measures have their limited use. The senses do not make for sense objects so long as a man is fasting, but fasting alone does not destroy his relish for them. On the other hand that relish may be heightened when the fast is broken, and a man can get rid of it only with the grace of God. The senses are so powerful that they drag a man behind them by force if he is not on his guard. Therefore a man must always keep them under control. This end he can achieve only if he turns his eyes inward, realizes God Who resides in his heart and is devoted to Him. One who thus looks upon Me as his goal and surrenders his all to Me, keeping his senses in control, is a yogi stable in spirit. On the other hand if a man is not master of his senses, he is always musing on the objects of sense and conceives an attachment for them, so that he can hardly think of anything else. From this attachment arises desire; and when the desire is thwarted he gets angry. Anger drives him nearly mad. He cannot understand what he is about. He thus loses his memory, behaves in a disorderly manner and comes to an ignoble end. When a man's senses rove at will, he is like a rudderless ship which is at the mercy of the gale and is broken to pieces on the rocks. Men should therefore abandon all desires and restrain their senses, so that these do not indulge in undesirable activity. The eyes then will look straight and that too only at holy objects; the ears will listen to hymns in praise of God or to cries of distress; hands and feet will be engaged in service. Indeed all the organs of sense and of action will be employed in helping a man to do his duty and making him a fit recipient of the grace of God. And once the grace of God has descended upon him, all his sorrows are at an end. As snow melts in the sunshine, all pain vanishes when the grace of God shines upon him and he is said to be stable in spirit. But if a man is not stable-minded, how can he think good thoughts? Without good thoughts there is no peace, and without peace there is no happiness. Where a stable-minded man sees things clear as daylight, the unstable man distracted by the turmoil of the world is as good as blind. On the other hand what is pure in the eyes of the worldly wise looks unclean to and repels the stable-minded man. Rivers continuously flow into the sea, but the sea remains unmoved; in the same way all sense objects come to the yogi, but he always remains calm like the sea. Thus one who abandons all desires, is free from pride and selfishness and behaves as one apart, finds peace. This is the condition of a perfect man of God, and he who is established therein even at the final hour is saved (literally, set free, *mukta*).

CHAPTER THREE

When Krishna had thus set forth the marks of identification for a *sthitaprajna* person, Arjuna received the impression that one had only to sit quietly in order to attain such a state, as Krishna had not made the slightest reference to any need for action on his part. He therefore asked Krishna, "It seems as if you hold that knowledge is superior to action. If so, why are you urging me to this terrible deed and thus confusing my mind? Please tell me clearly where my welfare lies."

Krishna replied: "O sinless Arjuna, since the beginning of time seekers have taken one or the other of two different paths. In one of these the pride of place is given to knowledge and in the other it is given to action. But you will find that freedom from action cannot be attained without action, that wisdom never comes to a man simply on account of his having ceased to act. Man does not become perfect merely by renouncing everything. Don't you see that every one of us is doing something or other all the time? Our very nature impels us to action. Such being the law of nature, one who sits with folded hands but lets his mind dwell on the objects of sense is a fool and may even be called a hypocrite. Rather than indulge in such senseless inactivity, is it not better that a man should control the senses, overcome his likes and dislikes, and engage himself in some activity or other without fuss and in a spirit of detachment? Do your allotted duty, restraining the organs of sense, for that is better than inaction. An idler will only meet his end the sooner for his idleness. But while acting, remember that action leads to bondage unless it is performed in a spirit of sacrifice. Sacrifice (*yajna*) means exerting oneself for the benefit of others, in a word, service. And where service is rendered for service's sake, there is no room for attachment, likes and dislikes. Perform such a sacrifice; render such service. When Brahma created the universe, He created sacrifice along with it, as it were, and said to mankind,

'Go forth into the world; serve one another and prosper. Look upon all creatures as gods. Serve and propitiate those gods, so that being pleased they will be gracious to you and fulfill your wishes unasked.' Therefore understand that whoever enjoys the fruits of the earth, without serving the people and without having first given them their share, is a thief. And he who enjoys them after having given all creatures their share is entitled to such enjoyment and is thus freed from sin. On the other hand, those who labor only for themselves are sinners and eat the fruit of sin. It is a law of nature that creatures are sustained by food, food production depends on the rains, and the rains descend on the earth on account of *yajna,* that is to say, the labor of all creatures. There is no rain where there are no creatures, and it does rain where they are there. All live by labor; none can remain idle and live, and if this is true of the lower forms of life, it is still more applicable to man. Action takes its origin from Brahma and Brahma from the imperishable *brahma*; therefore the imperishable brahma is present in all kinds of sacrifice or service. And whoever breaks this chain of mutual service is a sinner and he lives in vain.

"When a man enjoys peace of mind and contentment, it may be said that there is nothing left for him to do. He does not stand to gain by action or by inaction. He has no personal interests to serve; and yet he must not cease to offer sacrifice. Therefore do your duty from day to day without entertaining likes and dislikes and in a spirit of detachment. He who acts in such a spirit enjoys the beatific vision. Then again if even a selfless king like Janaka reached perfection, all the while working for the good of the people, how can you behave in a way different from his? Whatever a good and great man does, common people imitate. Take My own case for instance. I have nothing to gain by action, and yet ceaselessly do I pour myself out in action. Hence it is that people too go on working more or less. But what would happen if I ceased to work? The world would collapse if the sun, the moon and the stars ceased to move. And it is I who set them in motion and regulate their activity. But there is a difference between My attitude and the attitude of the common man. I act in the spirit of perfect detachment while he harbors attachment and works in his own interest. If a wise man like you ceased to act, others too

13

would do the same and their minds would be unsettled. Therefore do your duty without attachment, so that others might not cease to work and might gradually learn to work without attachment. Man is bound to work in obedience to and in conformity with his own nature. Only a fool thinks that he himself is the doer. To breathe is a part of man's nature; when an insect settles upon the eye, the eyelid moves of its own accord. And nobody says, "I take in the air" or "I move the eyelid." In the same manner why should not all human actions be performed in accordance with the qualities of nature? Why should there by any egoism about it? In order that a man may be able thus to act naturally and without attachment, the best thing for him to do is to dedicate all his actions to Me and perform them without egoism as a mere instrument in My hands. When a man thus gets over selfishness, all his actions are natural and free from taint and he escapes many a trouble. Actions then have no binding force for him. Action being natural, it is sheer egoism to outrage nature and to claim to be inactive. The victim of such egoism will externally appear not to act, but his mind is always active in scheming. This is worse than external activity and has all the greater binding force.

"As a matter of fact the senses feel attraction and aversion for their respective objects. For instance the ears like to hear some things and do not like to hear other things. The nose likes to smell the rose, and does not like to smell dirt. This is also true of the other organs of sense. Therefore what man has to do is not to submit to these two robbers, namely, attraction and repulsion. If one wishes to escape their attentions, he must not go about in search of action. He must not hanker after this today, that tomorrow and the other thing the day after. But he should hold himself ready to render for the sake of God such service as falls to his share. Thus he will cultivate within himself the feeling that whatever he does is in fact an act of God and not his own, and his egoism will be a thing of the past. This is *svadharma* (one's own duty). One must stick to svadharma, for it is the best for himself at any rate. *Paradharma* (another's duty) may appear to be better, but even so it should be looked upon as dangerous. *Moksha* (salvation) lies in embracing death while doing one's own duty."

When Krishna said that action performed by one who is free from likes and dislikes is sacrifice, Arjuna asked, "What is it that makes a man commit sin? Very often it seems as if he were driven to sin by some outsider against his own will."

Krishna replied: "The slave drivers in this case are *Kama* (desire) and *Krodha* (anger). These are like blood brothers. If desire is not satisfied, anger is the inevitable consequence. One who is the slave of desire and anger is said to be inspired by *rajoguna* (the quality of passion), which is man's greatest enemy and against which he has to fight day in, day out.

"As dust hides a mirror, smoke suffocates a fire and the womb covers the embryo, even so anger deprives knowledge of its luster and suffocates it. And desire is insatiable like fire, and, taking possession of man's senses, mind and intellect, knocks him down. Therefore first control your senses, and then conquer the mind. When you have done this, the intellect also will obey your orders. For though among the senses, the mind and the intellect, the mind is greater than the senses and the intellect is greater than the mind, the soul is the greatest of all. Man has no idea of his own strength or soul force, and tends to believe that the senses, the mind and the intellect are not amenable to his control. But when once he has gained confidence in soul force, everything else becomes easy as a matter of course. And desire, anger and their countless hosts hold no terror for him who has mastered the senses, the mind and the intelligence."

I call this chapter the key to an understanding of the *Gita*, and the gist of it is that life is given us for service and not for enjoyment. We have therefore to impart a sacrificial character to our lives. Intellectual assent to this proposition is only the first step, but such assent and conduct in terms of that assent are bound to rid our heart of its impurities in course of time. But what is real service? In order to obtain the right answer to this question, restraint of the senses is essential, as it gives us a clearer and clearer vision of the God of truth. Service rendered with selfish motives ceases to be sacrifice. Hence the urgent need for the spirit of detachment. When this is understood, all manner of controversies lose their meaning for us. "Did Krishna really ask Arjuna to kill his relatives? Could such killing ever be a part of one's duty?" Questions like these are set at rest forever. When detachment governs our actions, even the weapon raised in order to strike an enemy down falls out of our hand. But a mere pretense of detachment serves no useful purpose. If only we persevere in our effort, detachment may come to us, perhaps the very first day, or maybe only after a thousand years. We must not worry over the time this takes, for the effort carries within itself the seeds of success. We must however be on our guard and make sure that it is a genuine effort, and that there is no self-deception. And this is certainly possible for us all.

CHAPTER FOUR

The Lord says to Arjuna: "The yoga of selfless action which I commend to you is an ancient truth; I am not propounding any new doctrine. I have declared it to you, as you are my devoted friend, in order to heal the conflict in your mind. Whenever goodness weakens and evil grows from strength to strength, I incarnate Myself and protect the good and destroy the wicked. Those who are aware of this power (*maya*) of Mine are confident that evil is bound to go under. I am always by the good man's side. He never strays from the strait and narrow path and comes to Me at last, for he meditates on Me and hides himself in Me and thus is delivered from passion and anger and is purified by austerity and wisdom. As a man sows, so he reaps. None can escape from the operation of the laws I have made. I established the four *varnas* (classes, not castes) by the different distribution of qualities and actions. However I am not their author, for I do not desire the fruits of action and have nothing to do with the merit or demerit arising therefrom. This divine *maya* (course of action) is worth knowing. All activities prevalent in the world are subject to divine laws, and yet God is not defiled by them. Therefore He is and also is not their author. And a man who does likewise and acts in a spirit of detachment without being defiled by actions and by the yearning for their fruit is sure to be saved. In action he sees inaction and he understands at once what is wrong action. Wrong actions are all those that are inspired by desire and cannot be performed in the absence of desire, such for instance as theft, adultery and the like. These simply cannot be done in a spirit of detachment. Therefore those who do the duty that lies nearest without desire and scheming for the fruit of the action may be said to have burnt up their actions in the fire of wisdom (*jnana*). A man who has thus abandoned the attachment to the fruit of action is always contented, always independent. He has his mind under control. He gives up all his possessions. And his activity is natural like the bodily functions of a healthy individual. He is free from any pride or even consciousness that he is acting on his own. He has the realization that he is a mere instrument of the divine will. What does it matter whether he meets with success or with failure? He is neither elated by the one, nor unnerved by the other. All his work is done as a sacrifice (*yajna*), that is to say, as service to the world. He meditates upon God in all his actions and in the end comes to Him.

"There are many forms of sacrifice, the root of which lies in purity and service, such as, for instance, control of the senses, charity and *pranayama* (breath control) practiced with a view to self-purification. Knowledge of these can be acquired from a wise teacher (*guru*) through humility, earnestness and service. If anybody indulges in various activities which he thinks are yajna, without any understanding of what yajna is, he will only do harm to himself and to the world. It is therefore necessary that all actions should be performed intelligently. This wisdom (*jnana*) is not mere book learning. In it there is no room for doubt. It begins with faith and ends in experience. It enables a man to see all beings in himself and to see himself in God so that everything appears to him to be actually informed by God. Such wisdom effects the salvation of the worst of sinners. It releases the seeker from the bondage of action, so that he is not affected by its results. There is nothing else in the world so holy as this wisdom. Therefore try to obtain it with a heart full of faith in God and with the senses under control, so that you will enjoy perfect peace of mind."

The third, fourth and the following fifth chapter should be read together, as they explain to us what the yoga of selfless action (*anasakti*) is and what are the means of practicing it. If these three chapters are properly understood, the reader will have less difficulty in tackling what follows. The remaining chapters deal in detail with the ways and means of achieving anasakti. We should study the *Gita* from this point of view, and if we pursue this study we shall find without much trouble a solution of the problems which confront us from day to day. This calls for daily practice. Let everybody try it. If for instance he is angry, let him remember the verse dealing with anger and subdue that enemy. Supposing we heartily dislike somebody, or are impatient or gluttonous or in doubt as to whether we should do or should not do something or other, all these difficulties can be solved with the help of Mother *Gita* if we have faith in it and give it constant study. Our daily recitation of the *Gita* as well as this series of letters is a means to this end.

CHAPTER FIVE

Arjuna said: "You speak highly of knowledge, so that I am inclined to think that action is unnecessary. But then you also praise action, thus making me feel that unselfish performance of action is the thing to do. My mind will be at peace only if you tell me definitely which of the two is better."

The Lord replied: "*Sannyasa* means knowledge and *karma-yoga* means selfless action. Both of them are good, but if I had to choose between the two, I should say that *yoga* or selfless action is better. The man who does not hate anyone or anything, does not long for anything and is free from the pairs of opposites such as heat and cold, pleasure and pain, is a *sannyasi* (wise man, literally one who renounces the world), no matter whether he is or is not a performer of action. He easily casts off the chain that binds him. Only the ignorant speak of wisdom and action as different, not the learned. The fruit of both is the same; both lead to an identical goal. Therefore he who sees them as one, sees truly. The man of pure wisdom achieves his object by merely willing it, and has no need to perform an outward act. When the city of Mithila was on fire, others were bound to rush to it and fight the fire. But King Janaka contributed to this fight by his mental determination only, for his servants were ready to obey his commands. If he had run about with a water-pot to quench the fire, he would only have done harm; others would have stared at him and failed to perform their own duty, or at the most would have rushed here and there with a view to the King's safety. But it is not given to every one of us to become a Janaka at once. It is indeed a very difficult task to reach a Janaka-like state. Only one in a million can reach it as the fruit of service extending over many lives, and it is not a bed of roses either. As a man goes on performing selfless action, his thought grows from strength to strength and he resorts less and less to external action. But he is hardly conscious of this change, and he has not this change in view either. He is devoted only to service, with the result that his power of rendering service increases to such an extent that he hardly seems to rest from service. And finally his service is limited to thought alone, just as an object in extraordinary motion seems to be at rest. It is obviously improper to say that such a man does nothing. But this lofty state can, as a rule, be only imagined, and not experienced. Hence my preference for karmayoga. Millions derive the fruit of *sannyasa* (wisdom, literally "renunciation") from selfless action alone. They would fall between two stools if they tried their hand at sannyasa. If they take to sannyasa, it is very likely that they will become hypocrites, and as they have ceased to perform action, they are lost altogether. But a man who has purified himself by means of selfless action, who has his mind and his senses under control and who had identified himself with all beings, loving them as himself—such a man stands apart from action although he is acting all the time, and is not bound by it. He talks, he walks, he takes part in normal human activity, but his activity seems to be merely a function of his organs of sense, and he himself seems to be doing nothing. The bodily functions of a physically healthy person are natural and spontaneous. His stomach for instance functions independently of him; he has not to bother about its functioning. Similarly a spiritually healthy person, though acting through his body, is not tainted by it and may be said to be doing nothing. Therefore a man should dedicate all his actions to *Brahma* (God) and perform them on His behalf, so that in spite of his activity he does not earn either merit or demerit and is untouched by either, like a lotus leaf which is untouched by water."

Therefore a *yogi* (man of selfless action), performing action with the body, mind and understanding in a spirit of detachment and without egotism, purifies himself and enters into peace. The non-yogi, on the other hand, being attached to the fruit of action, is a prisoner bound by his own desires. The yogi lives blissfully in the city with nine gates, that is, his body, having renounced all actions by his mind, and realized that there is nothing at all that he himself is doing or getting done.

The man with a purified soul does not commit sin, nor does he do any meritorious deed. He who acts in a spirit of detachment, having destroyed his egotism and renounced the fruit of action, becomes a mere machine moving at the will and pleasure of the Master Mechanic or an instrument in the hands of God. The question, therefore, of his earning merit or demerit does not arise. On the other hand, the ignorant man is always counting his merit and demerit, and sinking deeper and deeper into the pit, so that in the end the only thing he has earned is demerit. But as regards the man who destroys his own ignorance by wisdom from day to day, his spontaneous actions grow purer and purer, and appear perfect and meritorious in the world's eyes. He sees all things with an equal eye. He is equi-minded towards a learned and humble *Brahma*(God)-knowing Brahmin, a cow, an elephant, a dog and a degraded human being who is worse than a beast. That is to say, he serves them all with equal devotion. He does not honor any one of them or treat another with contempt. The man of selfless action holds himself to be the world's debtor, and he repays what he owes to everyone else and does him full justice. Here on earth he takes the creation captive and is filled with the spirit of the Supreme. He is not elated if anybody does something pleasant; nor is he pained if foul abuse is poured upon him. The man attached to the world seeks happiness from outside himself. On the other hand, he who acts in a spirit of selfless detachment discovers the spring of eternal peace in himself, having withdrawn his mind from external objects. All sensual pleasures are a source of pain. One should resist the rush of desire, anger and the like. The selfless yogi is constantly engaged in doing good to all creatures. His mind is free from doubt. He is not of the world though he is in the world. He turns his eyes inward by means of *pranayama* (control of breath), etc., and conquers desire, fear and anger. He knows Me alone to be the supreme Lord of all, the Friend, and the recipient of sacrificial offerings and enters into My peace."

CHAPTER SIX

The Lord said: "The man who does his duty without any selfish desire for fruit may be called a sannyasi as well as a yogi. But he who abstains from action altogether is only an idler. The root of the matter is that one should not allow his mind to flit from one object of desire to another and from that to a third. He who would practice yoga, i.e., evenness of temper (*samatvam*), cannot but perform action. The man who has achieved such evenness of temper will be serene, because his mere thoughts are charged with the strength of action. A yogi is one who is not attached to the objects of sense or to action and whose mind has ceased to roam restlessly.

"A man can be saved or ruined by himself alone. Therefore he becomes his own friend or his own enemy as the case may be. To one who has subdued his mind, his soul is a friend; while the soul is an enemy for him who has failed to achieve self-control. The test for self-control is that heat and cold, pleasure and pain, honor and dishonor do not disturb one's inner serenity. He is a yogi who is a man of knowledge as well as experience, who is unwavering and master of his senses and to whom gold, stone and earth seem all alike. He regards with an equal eye friend and foe, sinner and saint. With a view to attaining this state a man should stabilize his mind, divest it of all sensual desires, and meditate in solitude on the Supreme Self. It is not enough to practice yogic *asanas* (postures), etc. In order to achieve evenness of temper, one must scrupulously keep the major observances (*vratas*), such as *brahmacharya* (chastity) and the like. A man who thus takes his place on a firm seat, keeps the observances and concentrates his mind on God, enters into perfect peace.

"This equanimity is not for one who overeats or merely fasts, nor for one who is too much addicted to sleep or to vigils. Its seeker has to keep a sense of proportion in all his actions, such as eating and drinking, sleeping and keeping awake. To overeat one day and fast the next day, to oversleep for a day and keep a vigil the next, to work hard for a day and pass the next in idleness is no characteristic of a yogi. The yogi is stable-minded at all times, and is without effort free from all desires. He is like an unflickering lamp burning in a windless place. He is not tossed to and fro by dramatic events on the world stage or by his own brain waves. Such mental poise can be acquired by slow but steady effort. The mind is fickle and restless, but it should be gradually stabilized, for one can have peace of mind only when he is firm of understanding. In order thus to stabilize the mind, he should constantly fix it on the soul. He will then see all beings in himself and himself in all beings, for he will see Me in all beings and all beings in Me. He who is absorbed in Me, and sees Me everywhere ceases to be himself, so that he is at all times attuned to Me irrespective of what he is doing, and is incapable of sin."

Yoga thus described seemed to Arjuna to be a tall order, and he exclaimed: "How is one to achieve such equanimity? The human mind is restless like a monkey, and as difficult to control as the wind. How is it to be curbed?"

The Lord replied: "You are right. But if a man earnestly sets about conquering attachment and aversion, yoga will not be difficult for him to practice. But it would be clear to you that it is not for one who cannot control his mind."

Then Arjuna posed another question: "Supposing a man has faith, but is lax in his effort and is thus unsuccessful in perfecting himself, what happens to him? Is he destroyed like a broken cloud in the sky?"

The Lord said: "Such a man of faith is never lost, for no one who takes the right path ever comes to an evil end. After death he lives for a time in some celestial world according to his merit and is then reborn on the earth into a holy family. But such a birth is difficult to obtain. He then regains the mental impressions developed in his former lives, and struggling harder for perfection, reaches the supreme goal. Thus making an assiduous effort some attain equanimity soon, while others do so after a number of lives in accordance with the measure of their faith and endeavor. This evenness of temper is superior to asceticism, to knowledge and to sacred rites, for these latter are after all only means to the end of equanimity. Do you therefore become even-minded and a yogi. And even among yogis hold him to be the best who dedicates his all to Me and worships Me alone in full faith."

Pranayama (control of breath) and *asanas* (yogic postures) are referred to appreciatively in this chapter, but we should remember that at the same time the Lord has stressed the need for *brahmacharya*, i.e., keeping the observances calculated to take us nearer and nearer to God. It should be clearly understood that the mere practice of asanas and the like can never take us to the goal of evenmindedness. Asanas and pranayama may be of some slight help in steadying the mind and making it single-purposed, provided that they are practiced to that end. Otherwise they are no better than other methods of physical training. They are very useful indeed as physical exercise and I believe that this type of exercise is good for the soul, and may be performed from a bodily standpoint. But I have observed that these practices do only harm when indulged in for the acquisition of supernormal powers (*siddhi*) and the performance of miracles. This chapter should be studied as a summary of the teaching in the preceding three chapters. It cheers us up in our spiritual struggle. We should never be downhearted and give up the endeavor to reach evenness of temper.

CHAPTER SEVEN

The Lord said: "O King, I will tell you how a man who devotes his whole mind to Me, takes refuge in Me and practices karmayoga can have perfect knowledge of Me free from the shadow of a doubt. I will declare to you this knowledge based on experience, which, having been known, nothing more here remains to be known. Hardly one from among thousands strives to acquire this knowledge, and perhaps one only of these strivers make a success of it.

"Earth, water, fire, air, ether, mind, intellect and egoism—this is the eightfold composition of My *prakriti* (nature). This is the lower nature; the other is higher nature, that is, life. This world is born of these two natures, that is to say, from the coming together of body and soul. Therefore I am the cause of the origin and destruction of all things. As pearls are strung on a thread, even so is the world held together by Me. Thus I am the taste in the waters, the light in the sun and the moon, the syllable "Om" in the Vedas, the sound in ether, the spirit of enterprise in man, the sweet smell of the earth, the brightness in fire, the life in all that lives, the austerity of ascetics, the intelligence of the intelligent, the pure strength of the strong, and the craving of all beings which does not run counter to righteousness. In short you should understand that all that belongs to the states of *sattva, rajas* and *tamas* (harmony, passion and sloth) proceeds from Me, and depends on Me alone. People deluded by these three qualities (*gunas*) do not recognize Me Who am imperishable. My Maya made of these qualities is hard to overcome. But those who take refuge in Me pass beyond this Maya, that is, the three gunas. Foolish evildoers cannot think of coming to Me even in their dreams. Being steeped in illusion, they roam in darkness and do not acquire knowledge. But the doers of good deeds worship Me. Some of them do so in order to obtain relief in their distress; others seek for knowledge of Me. A third group are inspired by a desire to get something for themselves while others worship Me with understanding, thinking it to be their duty. Worship of Me means service of My creation. This service is rendered by some because of their misery, by others in order to gain some advantage, by a third group out of curiosity as regards the outcome of such activity and by a fourth group who know what they are about and for whom service of others is something that they cannot do without. These last are My wise devotees, dearer to Me than all the rest of them. Or rather they know Me best and are nearest to Me. Their wisdom is the fruit of a quest extending over a number of lives, and when they have acquired this wisdom, they see nothing in the world except Me, Vasudeva. But those who are smitten by a variety of desires resort to other deities. I alone, however, am the giver of rewards commensurate with the devotion of each. The achievement too of these devotees of limited understanding is limited, but they rest content with it. These men in their ignorance imagine that they know Me through the senses. They do not realize that My imperishable and supreme form is beyond the reach of the senses and cannot be grasped with the hands, the ears, the nose, the eyes. Thus the ignorant do not recognize Me though I am the creator of all things. This is my *yogamaya* (creative power). Pleasure and pain are the necessary consequence of likes and dislikes and keep mankind under the influence of delusion. But those who have freed themselves from delusion and purified their thoughts and actions hold firmly to their vows and offer Me constant worship. They know Me in the form of perfect *Brahma* (the Absolute) as well as of individual selfs embodied as various kinds of creatures (*adhyatma*), and My creative action (*karma*). Those who thus know Me as the One who governs the material (*adhibhuta*) and the divine (*adhidaiva*) aspects and the sacrifices (*adhiyajna*) and have attained evenness of temper are released from the bondage of birth and death after they have died. For having acquired the knowledge of reality their mind ceases to dwell on trivialities and seeing the whole universe to be filled with the spirit of God, they are absorbed in Him."

CHAPTER EIGHT

Arjuna asked, "You spoke of *Brahma* (the Absolute), adhyatma, karma, adhibhuta, adhidaiva and adhiyajna, but I do not understand the meaning of all these words. Again you say that at the hour of death you are revealed to those who know you as adhibhuta etc. and have attained evenness of temper. Please explain all this to me."

The Lord replied, "*Brahma* is the imperishable supreme aspect of God, and *adhyatma* is the individual soul living in the body of all beings as the doer and the enjoyer. *Karma* is the process through which all beings come into existence, or in other words, the process of creation. *Adhibhuta* is Myself as the perishable body, and *adhiyajna* is the individual soul purified through sacrifice. Thus whether as the body or as the foolish soul or as the purified soul or as Brahma, it is I who am everywhere. And never doubt this, that he who meditates on Me in all these aspects at the hour of death, forgets himself, is careful of nothing and desirous of nothing will be united with Me. Whatever a man constantly dwells on in his mind and remembers at the time of death is realized by him. Therefore at all times you should remember Me and set your mind and heart upon Me and you will surely come to Me. You may say that it is hard thus to stabilize the mind. But you take it from Me that one can become single-minded by daily practice and constant endeavor, for as I told you just now, all embodied beings are in the essence Myself in various forms. For this he should prepare himself from the very first so that his mind does not go astray at the time of death, but is steeped in devotion, keeps the life force (*prana*) steady, and thinks only of Me as the omniscient, the ancient, the ruler, the subtle supporter of all and dispeller of ignorance like the sun which drives darkness away.

"This supreme state is known to the Vedas as *akshara* (the Imperishable) Brahma and is reached by sages who have freed themselves from likes and dislikes. All who desire to reach it observe *brahmacharya*, i.e., keep body, mind and speech under control and give up all objects of sense in these three ways. Men and women who die, having controlled the senses and uttering the sacred syllable Om and remembering Me as they depart, reach the supreme state. Their mind is never distracted by other thoughts, and when they have thus come to Me, they are not reborn into this painful condition. To come to Me is the only means of breaking the vicious circle of birth and death.

"Men measure time by the human span of a hundred years, and during that period do thousands of questionable deeds. but time is infinite. A thousand *yugas* (ages) make up the day of Brahma; compared with it a human day or even a hundred years of human life are as nothing. What is the use of counting such infinitesimal measures of time? Man's life is as only a moment in the infinite cycle of time. It is to us therefore to think of God alone to the exclusion of all else. How can we afford to run after momentary pleasures? Creation and dissolution have gone on unceasingly during Brahma's day and night and will do so in future too.

"Brahma who creates and dissolves beings is only an aspect of Me. He is the unmanifested which cannot be perceived by the senses. Beyond this unmanifested there is yet another unmanifested aspect of Mine of which I have spoken to you. He who reaches it is not reborn, for there is no day or night so far as this is concerned. This is a calm and immovable aspect, which can be realized only by single-minded devotion. It supports and pervades the whole universe.

"It is said that one who dies in the bright half of the month during *Uttarayana* (the northward movement of the sun from January to July) comes to Me if he is mindful of Me at last, and that he who dies in the dark half of the month during *Dakshinayana* (the southward movement from July to January) is reborn into the world. Uttarayana and the bright fortnight here may be interpreted to mean the path of selfless service; and Dakshinayana and the dark half of month mean selfishness. The path of service is the path of wisdom, and the path of selfishness is the path of ignorance. He who treads the path of wisdom is released from bondage of birth and death while he who takes the path of ignorance becomes a bond-slave. After having realized the difference between the two, who would be so foolish as to prefer to walk in the way of ignorance? All men should learn to discriminate between the paths, renounce all fruits of merit, act in a spirit of detachment and discharge their duty with all their heart and soul, and thus endeavor to reach the supreme state described by Me."

CHAPTER NINE

Having described the lofty state of a yogi in the last verse of the preceding chapter, the Lord now naturally proceeds to sing the glory of *bhakti* (devotion). For the yogi in terms of the *Gita* is neither a dry-as-dust man of knowledge, nor a devotee carried away by his own enthusiasm, but a selfless performer of action imbued with the spirit of wisdom as well as devotion. So the Lord said, "As you are free from hatred, I shall now tell you the secret of wisdom, a knowledge of which will contribute to your welfare. This is the holy knowledge above all other and is easy to translate into action. Those who have no faith in it fail to find Me. Men cannot perceive My unmanifested form by their senses; yet it pervades the universe. It supports the universe; the universe does not support it. Again in a sense it may be said that all these beings are not in Me, and I am not in them. Although I am the source of all beings and their sustainer, they are not in Me and I am not in them; for in ignorance they do not know Me and are not devoted to Me. Know this to be my divine mystery.

"But though it seems as if I am not in these beings, I am like the air moving everywhere. All creatures pass into My nature at the end of a cycle and are reborn at the beginning of creation. These acts are Mine, but they do not bind Me, for I act in a spirit of detachment and am indifferent as to the fruit they bear. These events happen as such is My nature. But people do not recognize Me in such a guise and deny My existence altogether. They entertain vain aspirations, perform vain actions and are full of ignorance, so that they can be said to partake of the nature of demons. But those who abide in the divine nature know and worship Me as the imperishable creator. They are firm in their determination. They are always striving for virtue, praising Me, and meditating on Me. Others again believe Me to be one or to be many. There are countless attributes of Me; therefore those who believe Me to be many think of different attributes as so many different faces of Mine. But one and all, they are My devotees.

"I am the intention to offer a sacrifice, I the sacrifice itself, I the offering made to the spirits of the fathers, I the herb, I the sacred verse (*mantra*), I the oblation, I the fire to which it is offered. I am the father of this world, I the mother, the supporter and the grandsire, the object of knowledge, the syllable Om, *Rigveda, Samveda* and *Yajurveda* (the three oldest sacred books of the Hindus—*tray*). I am the end of the pilgrim's path, the sustainer, the lord, the witness. I am the shelter, the lover, the origin, the dissolution, heat and cold, being and non-being. Those who perform the rites mentioned in the Vedas do so in order to gain their fruit. They may thus attain the world of heaven, but they have to return to the world of mortals and to die. But if a man meditates upon Me with an undistracted mind and worships Me alone, I bear all his burdens, supply all his needs and protect his possessions. Some others who worship other deities with faith in their hearts are victims of ignorance, but they are really worshipping Me for I am the lord of all sacrifices. However, they do not know Me in My comprehensive nature and therefore are unable to reach the supreme state. Worshippers of the gods go to the world of the gods, the ancestor worshippers to the world of the fathers and those who worship the spirits go to the spirits, while those who worship Me with the right approach come to Me. I accept the offering of love made by seekers, even if it be only a leaf or a flower. Therefore whatever you do, do it only as an offering to Me, so that your responsibility for the good and evil results will cease altogether. As you will have renounced all the fruits of action, there will be no more births and deaths for you. I am the same to all beings; none is hateful or dear to Me. But those who worship Me with devotion are in Me, and I am in them. This is not partiality but only the natural consequence of their devotion. Devotion indeed works wonders. He who worships Me in utter devotion becomes a saint even if he has been a sinner. As darkness vanishes before the sun, a man abandons his evil ways as soon as he comes to Me. Therefore know for certain that My devotee shall not perish. He becomes a man of religion and enters into My peace. Those who are born in the so-called lower castes and illiterate women, *vaishyas* and *shudras* (farmer and merchant castes) who take refuge in Me come to Me. It goes without saying that so do Brahmins and Kshatriyas who lead a holy life. Every devotee enjoys the fruit of his devotion. Therefore you who have been born in this unsubstantial world should worship Me and work out your salvation. Fix your mind on Me, be devoted to Me, offer your sacrifices for My sake, prostrate yourself before Me. And if you are intent on Me and reduce yourself to zero by attuning yourself to Me, you are sure to come to Me."

We learn from this chapter that devotion (*bhakti*) means attachment (*asakti*) to God. This is the royal road to the cultivation of a selfless spirit. Therefore we are told at the very beginning that devotion is the sovereign yoga and is easy to practice. It is easy to practice if it takes hold of our heart, but hard going if it does not. Hence it has been described as something for which we have to offer our life itself as the price. But he who has plunged into it enjoys perfect bliss though it scares the mere spectator. Sudhanva was laughing as he lay in the boiling oil while the bystanders were seized with terror and anxiety. The "untouchable" Nanda is said to have danced as he was tried by the ordeal of fire. We need not bother whether or not these are true stories. But the fact is that a man reaches such a state of calmness and imperturbability when he is absorbed in something or other. He forgets himself. But who would set his heart on anything except God? "Do not prefer the bitter nimba to sugarcane or the glowworm to the sun and the moon." The ninth chapter thus shows that renunciation of the fruit of action is impossible without devotion (*bhakti*). Its last verse sums up the whole chapter and in a word means, "Seeking nothing, give yourself utterly to Me."

CHAPTER TEN

The Lord said, "Hear once more what I say with a view to the welfare of devotees. Even gods and great sages do not know my beginning, for the very simple reason that I am without beginning myself and am the origin of the universe including gods and sages. The wise man who knows Me to be unborn and without beginning is liberated from all sins, for when he realizes Me as such and himself as My child or as part and parcel of Me, he overcomes the human liability to sin. Ignorance of one's real nature is the root of sin.

"As all beings derive from Me, so do the various natures distributed to them, such as for instance forgiveness, truth, joy and sorrow, birth and death, fear and fearlessness. Those who know all these to be My glorious manifestations easily become even-minded, as they cease to be egotistic. Their heart is fixed on Me. They dedicate their all to Me. I am the only subject of their conversation. They glorify Me and live in happiness and contentment. To these loving worshippers always aware of Me I grant the power of understanding, by means of which they come to Me."

Arjuna then praised the Lord, "You are the supreme Brahma, the highest abode, and the Lord. You yourself say that sages worship you as the First of the Gods, the Birthless, the All-pervading. O Lord, O Father, no one knows your real nature; it is known to you alone. Now please tell me your glorious manifestations, and explain to me how I may recognize you by meditation."

The Lord replied, "There is no end to My divine manifestations, but I shall name the chief of these only. I am the *atman* (soul) dwelling in the heart of all beings. I am the beginning, the middle and the end of them all. Of the Adityas I am Vishnu. Among the lights I am the light-giving sun. Of the *Maruts* (wind-gods) I am Marichi. Among the stars I am the moon. Of the

Vedas I am the *Samaveda*. Of the gods I am Indra. Of the sense organs I am the mind. Of beings I am consciousness. Of the Rudras I am Shankara (Shiva). Of the Yakshas and Rakshasas I am Kubera. Of the *Daityas* (demons) I am Prahlada. Of beasts I am the lion. Of birds I am the eagle. Indeed I am even the gambling of the cheats. Whatever good or evil happens in this world happens only by My permission. Realizing this, men should give up their pride and steer clear of evil, for I am the dispenser of the fruits of their good and bad deeds. You should realize that only a single fraction of Mine sustains the entire universe."

CHAPTER ELEVEN

Arjuna, asking the Lord for a favor, said, "O Supreme Lord, by teaching me the truth about the soul, you have dispelled my ignorance. You are All, the Creator and the Destroyer, being Imperishable yourself. If possible, please let me have a vision of your divine Form."

The Lord said, "There are thousands of my divine forms in various colors. The *Adityas*, the *Vasus* and the *Rudras* (types of gods)—all are unified in My body, as well as all things, animate and inanimate. But you cannot see this My form with those fleshly eyes. Therefore I give you divine sight with which to see Me."

Sanjaya said to Dhritarashtra, "O king, speaking thus to Arjuna, the Lord revealed to him His marvellous form which defies description. We see a single sun in the sky every day, but supposing a thousand suns were blazing in the sky, that glory of what Arjuna saw was more dazzling than their accumulated light. The ornaments and the weapons of that Form were similarly divine. Arjuna's hair then stood erect. And he spoke, shaking all over.

Arjuna said, "O God, I see every thing and everybody within your body. Brahma and Shiva are there, and so are the sages and the holy serpents. I see you with countless arms and faces, and find no beginning, middle or end. You shine like a mass of insufferable light, and blaze like fire. You are the ultimate foundation of the universe, the Ancient of Days, and the guardian of eternal law. Wherever I look, I see parts of your body. The sun and the moon are your eyes as it were. You pervade heaven and earth. Your splendor burns up the universe. This world is seized with awe. The gods, the sages, and the siddhas—all are standing with clasped hands and sing your praise. On seeing this stupendous form and brilliance I lose my nerve. My patience and peace are gone. O God, have mercy on me. I see these men rush into your mouth frightful with tusks as moths fly into a flame and you crush them to powder. Who are you with such an awful form? I cannot understand your ways."

The Lord said, "I am Time, the destroyer of worlds. You may or may not fight, but the warriors on both the sides are bound to perish. You are only an instrument of the divine will."

Arjuna said, "O God, home of all the world, you are the Imperishable, being and non-being and what is beyond either of them. You are the First of the gods, the Ancient of Days; you are the refuge of the world. You are the one thing which is to be known. You are *Vayu* (wind), *Yama* (the God of death and judgment), *Agni* (fire) and *Prajapati* (the Creator). Hail to you a thousand times. Now please show me your original form again."

The Lord then said, "I showed My world-wide form to you, because I love you. You have seen today something the vision of which cannot be won by Vedic or any other studies, rituals, alms or austerities. Do not be bewildered because you have seen it. Cast away fear, be calm and see My familiar form. That shape of mine which you have seen is hard to see even for the gods and can be seen only by pure devotion. Whoever works for Me, makes Me his supreme good, becomes My devotee, frees himself from attachment and loves all beings, comes to Me."

I have deliberately cut this as well as the last chapter short. This one is full of poetry and therefore should be read frequently either in the original or in translation, so that we may be imbued with the spirit of devotion. Whether we are or not thus imbued can be found by applying the acid test mentioned in the last verse. Devotion is impossible in the absence of total self-surrender and all-embracing love. Self-surrender and a sense of solidarity with all living beings become easy of attainment if we meditate on God as world-destroying time into whose gaping mouths the universe rushes to its doom. This fate is bound to overtake us too all of a sudden, whether we wish for it or not. Thus all distinctions of small and big, high and low, man and woman, men and the lower animals disappear. Seeing that we are all a mere morsel in the mouth of God as the Destroyer, we should become humble and reduce ourselves to zero and cultivate friendship with everyone else. If we do this, we shall cease to be afraid of this terrible Form of God. On the other hand it will give us peace of mind.

CHAPTER TWELVE

I propose today to give the substance of Chapter Twelve, which deals with devotion (*bhakti*). Whenever there is a wedding in the Ashram, we ask the couple to learn by heart and ponder over this chapter as one of the five sacrifices they have to offer. Knowledge and action in the absence of devotion are dry as dust and are likely to make us confirmed bond-slaves. Let us therefore commence this study of the *Gita* with a heart full of devotion.

Arjuna asks the Lord, "Some devotees adore a personal (*sakara*) God while others worship the Absolute (*nirakara*). Which of these two courses is better?"

The Lord replies, "Those who fix their minds on Me (as the One Life in all) with perfect faith and are absorbed in Me are My devotees indeed. But those who worship the Absolute and restrain and subdue their senses, are equiminded towards all living beings and serve them without looking on some as of a superior and others as of an inferior grade—they also will come to Me. Neither of these two classes of devotees is superior to the other. But a full realization of the Absolute is almost impossible for an embodied being. The Absolute is devoid of all attributes and thus difficult for men even to imagine. Therefore they are all worshippers of a personal God, whether they are aware of it or not.

"Do you therefore place your mind in Me (the personal God in the universal form) and offer Me your all. If this is not possible, try to restrain the aberrations of the mind; that is to say, by observing the yamas and niyamas, and with the help of pranayama and yogic exercises, obtain control over the mind. If even this is beyond your capacity, perform all actions for My sake, so that your delusion will be destroyed, and you will be imbued with the spirit of detachment and devotion. If you cannot do even this, renounce the fruits of action, that is, cease to have a desire for the fruits of action, and do the task which is allotted to you. A man can never have any say as regards the fruit of his action, as the nature of the fruit is determined by a number of independent factors. Be you therefore a mere instrument in My hands. I have thus described four methods, none of which is superior to the others. You may adopt any one of the four you like. It may seem as if the path of knowledge (hearing the doctrine, pondering over it, etc.) is easier to take than that of yamas, niyamas, pranayama, asanas, etc., meditation in worship is easier still and the renunciation of the fruit the easiest of all. But the same method is not equally well suited for all. And some seekers have to adopt all the four methods, which are interconnected. You must become a devotee one way or other; you may take any path that leads to this destination.

"Let me tell you what the true devotee is like. He does not hate or bear ill will to any living creature. He looks on all with love and compassion. He is free from the delusion of "I" and "Mine." He reduces himself to zero. Pleasure and pain are equally acceptable to him. He forgives the wrong-doer even as he expects to be forgiven himself. He is always contented with his lot, and is unshakable in his resolve. He dedicates his intellect and mind and all to Me. He never molests his fellow-creatures; these are therefore never afraid of him. He does not allow himself to become perturbed by the world. He is free from exultation, sorrow, anger, fear and the like. He seeks nothing for himself. He is pure and skillful in action. He renounces every undertaking. Although he is firm in his resolve, he is indifferent as regards the success or failure of his action; that is to say, he is not anxious about its result. He is alike to friend and foe. Honor and insult are the same to him. He is silent and content with what comes. He moves freely as if he were alone. He has a steady mind at all times and places. A devotee who behaves like this in faith is dear to me."

Q. The devotee "renounces all undertakings." What does this mean?

A. The devotee will not draw up schemes of future expansion. For example, if a merchant who deals in cloth now has any plans of selling firewood as well in the future, or if he, having one shop only, thinks of opening five more shops, that would be *arambha* (undertaking) on his part, and the devotee will have none of it. This principle is applicable to service of the nation as well. For instance a worker in the khadi department today will not take up cowkeeping tomorrow, agriculture the day after and medical aid on the fourth day. He will do his best in whatever has come to him. When I am free from egoism, nothing remains for me to do.

The Lord has bound me with a cotton thread; I am His, no matter where He leads me. I have been stabbed with the dagger of love." A devotee's every activity is planned by God. It comes to him as in the natural course of things. He therefore rests content with, "this, that or anything else." This is the meaning of "renouncing all undertakings." The devotee does not cease to work; indeed he is nothing if not a worker. He only ceases to think needless thoughts about his work. It is these that he has to renounce.

"This has been acquired by me today; that purpose I shall gain tomorrow"—this is the opposite of "renouncing undertakings."

CHAPTER THIRTEEN

The Lord said, "*Kshetra* (the Field) is another name for the human body and *Kshetrajna* means one who knows the Field. Understand Me as the Knower of the Field in all bodies. Real knowledge means discrimination between the Field and the knower of the Field. The five great elements, namely, earth, water, fire, air and ether, individuality (*ahamkara*), intellect, the unmanifest, the ten senses (the five organs of perception: hearing, touch, sight, taste, and smell; and the five organs of action: tongue, feet, hands, and the organs of evacuation and reproduction), mind, the five sense objects, desire and hatred, pleasure and pain, *sanghata* (the power of combination inherent in the constituents of the body), consciousness and cohesion—these constitute the Field with its modifications. Knowledge of these is essential, as they have to be renounced. Wisdom is the foundation on which such renunciation can be based. Wisdom here means and includes humility, unpretentiousness, non-violence, forgiveness, rectitude, service of the teacher, purity, steadfastness, self-restraint, indifference to sense objects, absence of egoism, insight into the evil of birth, death, old age, disease and pain, detachment from wife and children, hearth and home, friends and relations, equimindedness to good and bad fortune, wholehearted devotion to God, love of solitude, dislike for the enjoyment of sensual pleasures in company with others, thirst for knowledge of the soul, and at last the beatific vision. And the reverse of this is ignorance. Now let me tell you something about that which has to be known with a view to salvation. That is beginningless supreme Brahma. Brahma is beginningless because it is unborn and was there when there was nothing. It is neither *sat* (existent) nor *asat* (non-existent) but beyond them both. But from another standpoint it can be called sat, because it is eternal. Human beings cannot recognize it as such; therefore it is said to be beyond even sat. It pervades the whole universe. It may be said to have a thousand hands and feet, and though it seems to have hands and feet, it is devoid of the organs of sense for it does not need these organs. Sense organs are transitory while Brahma is eternal. And although, being all-pervasive and all-sustaining, it may be said to be enjoying the qualities (*gunas*), it is free from them. Where there are gunas, there is change (*vikara*), but Brahma is changeless. It may be said to be outside all beings, because it is out for those who do not know it. And it is within all beings as it is all-pervading. Similarly it is both moving and unmoving. It is subtle and hence imperceptible. It is distant as well as near. It is undivided in the sense that it is imperishable though name (*nama*) and form (*rupa*) perish, but it also seems to be divided as we say that it is within all creatures. It creates, preserves and destroys. It is the light of lights beyond darkness, and the end of all knowledge. Brahma which is planted in every heart is *jneya*, the one thing worth knowing. All knowledge is a means to the end of being united with it.

"God and His *maya* (nature) are both without beginning. Modifications (*vikaras*) are born of maya and these give rise to various kinds of action (*karma*). On account of maya, the soul experiences pleasure and pain and the fruit of merit (*punya*) and demerit (*papa*). He who, having realized this, does his duty in a spirit of detachment is not born again in spite of his activity, for he beholds the face of God in all faces, and, seeing that not a leaf moves but by the divine will, he is free from egotism, understands that he is separate from the body and that the soul, though living in the body, remains by means of knowledge unaffected like the omnipresent ether."

CHAPTER FOURTEEN

The Lord said, "Once more I will teach you the supreme wisdom which enabled sages to reach the highest perfection. People who find that wisdom and do their duty accordingly are delivered from the cycle of births and deaths. O Arjuna, know Me to be the father and mother of all beings. The three gunas born of nature, viz., *sattva* (goodness), *rajas* (passion) and *tamas* (ignorance) bind the soul down. They may be described respectively as the highest, the middling and the lowest. Of these, sattva is pure and unsullied and gives light; it is therefore the source of happiness. Rajas arises from attachment and craving and makes a man indulge in all manner of activities. Tamas is rooted in ignorance and delusion and makes one negligent and indolent. In short sattva makes for happiness, rajas for restlessness and tamas for sloth. Sometimes sattva prevails, overpowering rajas and tamas; at other times rajas prevails, overpowering sattva and tamas; at still other times tamas prevails, overpowering sattva and rajas. When the light of wisdom shines through all the activities of the body it may be known that sattva is increasing. Where greed, bustle, unrest and competition are observed, rajas is the ruler. And the predominance of tamas is characterized by ignorance, sloth and delusion. If sattva prevails in a man's life, he is born in the sinless worlds of the great sages after death. If rajas dominates his life, he is born among those who are attached to action. And if tamas is the ruling principle, he returns to the womb of the senseless. The fruit of *sattvika* action is purity, while the fruit of rajas is pain and the fruit of tamas is ignorance. A sattvika man rises to the higher regions; a *rajasa* man remains in this world, while a *tamasa* man sinks to the underworld. When a man perceives no doer of action other than these qualities and knows Me who am beyond them he enters into My nature. When the dweller in the body has overcome the three qualities from which all bodies arise, he is freed from birth and death, old age and pain and drinks the nectar of eternal life."

On hearing that one who transcends the qualities makes such great progress on the pilgrim's path, Arjuna asked, "What are the marks of such perfection? How does such a perfect being conduct himself? And how does he cross over the qualities?"

The Lord replied, "A man is said to have risen above the qualities when he is not angry if the light and knowledge of sattva or the activity and bustle of rajas or the delusion and ignorance of tamas are there and is not wishful if they are not. He sits like one who is unconcerned and is not disturbed by the qualities. He stands apart unmoved, being aware that they are the doers of all actions. He is even-minded to pleasure and pain as well as to a lump of earth, a stone and gold. The pleasant and the unpleasant are alike to him. He is unaffected by either praise or blame. He is the same in honor and evil fame. He is alike to friend and foe. And he has abandoned all undertakings.

"Do not think that this is a goal you can never reach and that therefore you need not exert yourself. What I have described is the state of a perfect man. The way to it is to serve Me with single-minded devotion. From the third chapter onwards I have pointed out that a man cannot so much as even breathe without action (*karma*), from which no human being can ever hope to escape. He who would transcend the qualities should dedicate all his actions to Me, and cease to desire their fruits. If he does this, his actions will not be an impediment to his progress, for I am Brahma, immortal life, the eternal law and joy forever.

"When a man reduces himself to zero, he sees Me alone everywhere. He is *guna-atita* (one who has crossed over the qualities)."

CHAPTER FIFTEEN

The Lord said, "This world is like an *ashvattha* (sacred fig) tree with roots above and branches below and with the Vedic hymns as its leaves. And he who knows it knows the Vedas. The branches of this cosmic tree nourished by the qualities "shoot to heaven and sink to earth" (Sir Edwin Arnold). Sense objects are its sprouts. It is these things of the senses which bind the soul with the bonds of karma in the world of men.

"The real nature of this tree cannot be known here, nor its beginning, nor end, or foundation.

"This strongly rooted cosmic tree should be cut down with the weapon of non-cooperation, so that the soul may rise to a higher world from which there is no return to the world of mortals. With this end in view a man should engage himself in the constant worship of the Ancient of Days, from whom all this activity (the cosmic process) seems to flow. The wise man who is free from pride and delusion, victorious over the vice of attachment and devoted to the Supreme Soul, who is free from cravings and to whom pleasure and pain are alike—that wise man reaches the state which is beyond all change, and which does not need to be illumined by the sun, the moon or fire. That is My supreme abode.

"An eternal part of Myself transformed into the individual soul in this world draws to itself the senses including the mind which reside in matter. When the soul enters the body or leaves it, it takes these senses with it even as the wind carries fragrance from its places. It enjoys sense objects with the help of the ear, the eye, the senses of touch and taste, the nose and the mind. The ignorant cannot recognize it as it goes or stays or enjoys itself under the influence of the qualities, but the sages see it with the eye of wisdom. Striving yogis see it living in their own bodies, but those who have not achieved evenness of temper cannot see it even if they try.

"The light of the sun that illumines the world, that which is in the moon and in fire—know that all that light is Mine. Permeating the soil I sustain all living beings. I become the sap-producing moon and feed the plants. Becoming the fire of life in the bodies of all living creatures and being united with the life breaths, I digest the four kinds of food. I abide in all hearts. From Me are memory and wisdom as well as their absence. I am that which is to be known by all the Vedas. So also I am the author of Vedanta and the knower of the Vedas.

"There may be said to be two kinds of personalities in this world, namely *kshara* (the perishable) and *a-kshara* (the imperishable). The perishable is all beings; and the imperishable is I who inspire them, and am the same for ever. But beyond either is the highest spirit who is called the Supreme Soul, and who, pervading all, sustains the three worlds. This too is I. I therefore transcend the perishable and even the imperishable, and am known in the world as well as in the Vedas as the supreme reality. The wise man who recognizes Me as such knows all that need be known, and serves Me with his whole being.

"O sinless Arjuna, I have told you this secret teaching. By knowing this a man becomes truly wise and reaches the shores of salvation."

CHAPTER SIXTEEN

The Lord said, "I will now point out the distinction between the divine and the demoniacal natures. Among the signs of the divine are fearlessness, purity of heart, wisdom, evenness of temper, self-control, almsgiving, sacrifice, study of the scriptures, austerity, straightforwardness, non-violence, truth, freedom from anger, renunciation, peacefulness, not speaking evil of others, compassion to all living beings, absence of greed, gentleness, modesty, absence of fickleness, vigor, forgiveness, fortitude, purity, internal as well as external, freedom from malice and pride.

"Among the signs of the demoniacal are hypocrisy, arrogance, conceit, anger, cruelty and ignorance.

"The divine nature leads to liberation while the demoniacal leads to bondage. O Arjuna, you are born with the endowments of the divine nature.

"I will say something more about the demoniacal nature, so that people may easily give it up. Men of such a nature do not know what to do and what to refrain from doing. There is no purity or truth in them, so that they do not observe the rules of good conduct.

"They hold that the world is unreal, without basis or ruler. For them sex is all the world so that they think of nothing except enjoyment of the objects of sense.

"They do horrible deeds. They are dull-witted. They hold fast to their wicked thoughts and all their activity is directed only to the destruction of the world. Their desires are insatiable. They are full of hypocrisy, pride and arrogance. They are thus plagued by innumerable cares. They want fresh sensual pleasures every day. They are 'ensnared / In nooses of a hundred idle hopes' (Edwin Arnold, *Light of Asia*), and by unlawful means amass wealth in order to gratify their desires.

" 'I got this today; I will get that tomorrow. I killed this one enemy today; I will also kill others. I am a man of might. I have great possessions. Who is my equal? With a view to fame I will sacrifice to the gods, give alms and make merry.' They say this to themselves with a chuckle, and, being caught in the net of delusion, go to hell at last.

"Men with such nature, given over to pride, speak ill of others and thus hate God who dwells in all hearts. They are therefore frequently born in the wombs of degraded parents.

"There are three gates to hell, leading to the ruin of the soul: lust, anger and greed. Therefore we should renounce them all. Turning aside from them, men go by the strait and narrow path and reach the highest state.

"He who disregards the scriptures composed of eternal principles and gives himself up to pleasure cannot attain happiness or peace characteristic of the right way.

"Therefore in deciding what you must do and what you must not do, you should acquire the knowledge of fundamental and immutable principles from wise men and think and act accordingly."

CHAPTER SEVENTEEN

Arjuna asked, "What happens to those who serve in faith, neglecting the prevailing code of conduct?"

The Lord replied, "There are three kinds of faith, characterized by sattva, rajas or tamas as the case may be. As is a man's faith, so is he.

"*Sattvika* men worship the gods; *rajasa* men worship demigods and demons; and *tamasa* men worship the spirits of the dead.

"The nature of a man's faith cannot be ascertained offhand. In order to assess it correctly one must know the precise nature of his food, austerity, sacrifice and alms-giving.

"Foods which make for long life and increase the vital force, energy, strength and health are said to be *sattvika*. *Rajasa* foods are violently bitter, sour, hot or pungent and give rise to disease and aches and pains. And cooked food which is stale or gives out a bad smell and the leavings of others are said to be *tamasa*.

"The sacrifice which is offered as a matter of duty without expecting a reward and with mental concentration is said to be sattvika. A rajasa sacrifice is that in which a reward is desired and which is offered for outward show. And a tamasa sacrifice is one in which scriptural rules are disobeyed, no eatables or alms are given away and no hymns are chanted.

"Honoring the saintly, purity, brahmacharya and non-violence constitute austerity of the body. Truthful, pleasant and beneficial speech as well as a study of the scriptures is austerity of the speech. And cheerfulness, gentleness, silence, self-control and purity of motive—these are called the austerity of the mind. Such austerity of the mind, body and speech as is practiced without desire of fruit by men with an evenness of temper is said to be *sattvika*. Austerity practiced for ostentation and with a view to gaining honor is said to be *rajasa*. And austerity done by obstinate fools with self-torture or with the object of hurting others is said to be *tamasa*.

"A gift 'made in due place, due time and to a fit recipient' without expecting reward and with a feeling that it is right for a man to give is said to be sattvika. A gift made grudgingly with a view to getting something in return is regarded as rajasa. And the gift which is given in a contemptuous spirit, and without honor done to the recipient and without considering the proper time and place for it is said to be tamasa.

"Brahma is designated in the Vedas as *Om tat sat*. Therefore men of faith pronounce the sacred syllable *Om* when they commence any rite of sacrifice, alms-giving or austerity. This single syllable stands for Brahma. *Tat* means that. And *sat* means *satya*, beneficent. That is to say, God is one, He alone is, He alone is truth and the benefactor of the world. He who offers a sacrifice, makes gifts or practices austerity with a realization of this truth and in a spirit of dedication is a man of sattvika faith. And he is free from blame if he knowingly or unknowingly does something different from the correct procedure in the spirit of dedication. But acts undertaken in the absence of such a spirit are said to be performed without faith and therefore are *asat* (unreal)."

CHAPTER EIGHTEEN

Even after he had pondered over the teaching in all the previous chapters, there was still a doubt in Arjuna's mind. So he said, "The sannyasa of the *Gita* seems to be different from renunciation as currently understood. Are sannyasa and tyaga really different?"

While resolving Arjuna's doubt in answer to this question, the Lord summarized the *Gita* doctrine in a concise manner: "Some actions are motivated by desire. Various activities are indulged in by men with a view to fulfill various desires. These are called *kamya* actions. Then again there are certain necessary and natural actions such as breathing, eating, drinking, lying down, sitting, etc., with a view to keep the body a fit instrument of service. And thirdly there are actions done with a view to serve others. Giving up kamya actions is *sannyasa*, and renunciation of fruits of all actions is *tyaga* as recommended to you all along.

"Some people maintain that there is evil, no matter how little, in all actions whatever. Even so, a man must not give up actions done with a view to *yajna* (sacrifice), that is to say, the service of others. Alms-giving and austerity are included in yajna. But even while serving others, a man should act in a spirit of detachment. Otherwise his activity is likely to be mixed up with evil.

"Renunciation owing to ignorance of duties that must be done is said to be inspired by tamas. Giving up any action merely because it involves physical suffering is said to be rajasa. But service rendered to others because of a feeling that it must be done and without the desire for the fruits is real *sattvika tyaga*. In this tyaga therefore there is no giving up of all actions, but only of the fruit of duties that must be done, and of course of other, that is, kamya, actions. When a wise man acts in such a selfless spirit, all his doubts are dispelled, his motives are pure and he has no thought of personal comfort and discomfort.

"He who does not abandon the fruits of action must enjoy or put up with the natural consequences of his own acts, and is thus a bond-slave forever. But he who gives up the fruits of action achieves freedom.

"And why should a man feel attachment for action? It is idle for anybody to imagine that he himself is a doer. There are five causes for the accomplishment of all actions, namely, this body, the doer, the various instruments, efforts, and last but by no means the least, providence.

"Realizing this, a man should give up pride. He who does something without egoism may be said to be not doing it in spite of his doing it, for he is not bound by his action. Of a humble person who has reduced himself to zero it may be said that he does not kill though he kills. This does not mean that the man in spite of his humility may kill, and yet be unaffected by the killing. For no occasion can arise for such a man to indulge in violence.

"There are three things that inspire action: knowledge, the object of knowledge and the knower. And there are three constituents of action: the organ, the deed and the doer. The thing to be done is the object of knowledge; the method of doing it is knowledge and he who knows it is the knower. After he has thus received an impulse to action, he performs an action in which the senses serve as instruments. Thought is translated into action.

> *That by which a man is able*
> *To see one changeless Life in all the lives*
> (Edwin Arnold)

and to realize the essential unity that underlies all diversities is sattvika knowledge. In rajasa knowledge one holds that there are different souls in different creatures, while in tamasa knowledge a man does not know a thing and imagines that everything is mixed up without rhyme and reason.

"Similarly there are three kinds of action. Action in which there are no likes and dislikes and no desire for personal gains is sattvika. That in which there are a desire for enjoyment, egoism and restlessness is rajasa action. And tamasa action is one in which no thought at all is given to personal capacity and consequential injury or violence and which is undertaken through delusion.

"So also there are three classes of doers. A sattvika doer is free from attachment and egoism and yet firm and enterprising and is neither elated by success nor worried by failure. A rajasa doer is impassioned, greedy and violent, 'slave by turns of sorrow and of joy' (Edwin Arnold) and of course desires to obtain the fruit of his actions. And a tamasa doer is unsystematic, procrastinating, obstinate, malicious and indolent; in short, without an iota of self-culture.

"Intellect, firmness and happiness also are said to be of three kinds.

"The sattvika intellect is able properly to distinguish between action and non-action,

> *What must be done, and what must not be done,*
> *What should be feared, and what should not be feared*
> *What binds and what emancipates the soul.*
> (Edwin Arnold)

The rajasa intellect tries to draw these distinctions but generally fails to do so correctly, while the tamasa intellect 'looks upon right and sees all things contrariwise of truth' (Edwin Arnold).

"Firmness is the power of taking up something and sticking to it through thick and thin. It is more or less inherent in all things; otherwise the world could not subsist for a single moment. Firmness is sattvika when there is a constantly maintained balance between the activities of the mind, the vital airs (*pranas*) and the senses. The firmness by which a man holds fast to duty, pleasure and wealth from attachment and with a view to personal advantage is rajasa. And firmness is tamasa,

> *... wherewith the fool*
> *Cleaves to his sloth, his sorrow and his fears,*
> *His vanity and despair.*
> (Edwin Arnold)

"Sattvika happiness is the

> ...*pleasure that endures,*
> *Banishing pain for aye, bitter at first*
> *As poison to the soul, but afterwards*
> *Sweet as the taste of Amrit.*
>   (Edwin Arnold)

"It arises from true self-knowledge.

> *Rajasa happiness arises from sensual enjoyment.*
> ...*Sweet*
> *As Amrit is its first taste, but its last*
> *Bitter as poison.*
>   (Edwin Arnold)

"And tamasa happiness is that

> ...*which springs*
> *From sloth and sleep and foolishness.*
>   (Edwin Arnold)

"This threefold classification is thus applicable to all things. The duties of the four *varnas* (classes in ancient Hindu society) are fixed by reason of the dominance or recession of the qualities planted in each.

"A *Brahman*'s conduct is characterized by calmness, self-discipline, austerity, purity, forgiveness, uprightness, wisdom, experience and faith in God. The characteristics of a *Kshatriya* are valor, splendor, firmness, resourcefulness, not flying from battle, open-handedness and leadership. A *Vaishya*'s task is 'to till the ground, tend cattle, venture trade' (Edwin Arnold), and service is the *Shudra*'s work. This is not to say that a member of any one of these classes may not be endowed with qualities characteristic of other classes or is not entitled to cultivate them in himself. But qualities and work as mentioned above serve as signs for the recognition of a man's varna. If the qualities and tasks of each caste are recognized, there is no undesirable competition or feeling of hatred among them. There is no question here of high and low. But if each does his duty selflessly according to his nature, he will reach perfection. Therefore one's own duty, though it appears to be valueless, is better than the duty of another which seems to be easy. A man may remain free from sin when he performs the task naturally allotted to him, as he is then free from selfish desires; the very wish to do something else arises from selfishness. For the rest, all actions are clouded by defects as fire by smoke. But the natural duty is done without desire for its fruit, and thus loses its binding force.

"The calm yogi who has been sanctified by thus performing his own duty, who has his mind under control, who has given up the five sense objects, who has overcome likes and dislikes, who lives in solitude, i.e., whose eyes are turned inward, who achieves mastery of his mind, body and speech by abstemiousness, who is ever conscious of the living presence of God, and who has given up pride, desire, anger, acquisitiveness and the like—that yogi is fit to be united with Brahma. He is equiminded towards all men. He neither rejoices nor indulges in grief. Such a devotee has true knowledge of God and is absorbed in Him. Thus taking refuge in Me, he gains the eternal place.

"Therefore dedicate your all to Me, regard Me as the supreme object of your love, and with discrimination, fix your mind on Me. As you do this, you will overcome all difficulties. But if out of egoism you do not listen to Me, you will perish. The one thing needful is that, abandoning all conflicting views, you should come to Me alone for shelter, and thus be freed from sin.

"Do not tell this truth to anyone who is not a devotee, austere in life, and, hating Me, does not wish to listen. But one who communicates this great secret to My devotees will surely come to Me in virtue of his devotion."

After having thus reported to Dhritarashtra the dialogue between Arjuna and Krishna, Sanjaya said, "Where there is Krishna, the prince of yoga, and Arjuna with his bow and arrows, there are prosperity, victory, happiness and fundamental morality."

Krishna, to whom the epithet "prince of yoga" has here been applied, means pure knowledge based on spiritual experience, and by referring to Arjuna as an archer it is suggested that where there is action in accordance with such knowledge, the doer obtains every wish that is not contrary to lofty morals.